The NOISY Snails

Written By: Michael J. Myers
Illustrated By: Richard Wright

While I never intended to sit down and begin writing children's books, for I am a 23-year-old MotorHead, the idea came to me one day and has consumed me ever since. The Noisy Snails started as a vision that worked its way into a book, and then into a series of books: The Motorhead Garage Series.

Enjoy!

"Shhhwushhhhhh chuwww..."

"Daddy, Daddy, WAKE UP!"

"Shhhwushhhhhh chuwww Shhwushhhh chuwww..."

"DAD, WAKE UP!"

"Shhhwushh chuwww Shhwushhhhhh chuwww..."

"SHHHWUSHHHH CHUWWW SHWUSHHH..."

...WOMP WOMP
POP POP POP
POP POP
Chuwww ..."

"Boys, Boys! TURN YOUR BOOST DOWN! There is no need to 2step this early. I'm up! I'm up!"

"Dad, it's race day!"

The Twins were awake
and warming their motor.
Fillin' up the garage
with exhaust odor.

The boys couldn't hold back.

Their new shells were waiting at the track!

After a scrub down and a rinse,
the Twins were ready to cruise.

Papa jacked the boys up
and bolted on their racing shoes.

At Motorhead Raceway, the sun was shining.

The tires were **chirping** and the motors were **whining.**

"Brrrumpppp whinee
whineeeeee.
Brrrumpppp
whinnnnee whineeeeeeee."

"Brrrumpppp whinnnne whineeeeee."

"Hey look!
Walter got his belt! He is now a
full **Supercharger!**

"DAD, can we get our shells?? Can we PLEASE?"

The boys begged...

Papa took the boys to Pit Stop Joe
for an introduction.
What he had was race worthy
forced induction.

"Here ya go Laggy,
the Twins will sure make
a lot more boost with these."

"Alright boys. Pull up nice and slow..."

chirped Pit Stop Joe.

"Vroomm Chushhhhhh.
Vroomm
Chuuuueeee."

Pit Stop Joe finished replacing the Twin's stock shells with aftermarket racing shells.

It was about time for some good clean fun... the Twins were now ready for a test run.

The empty side of the parking lot looked like the perfect spot.

"Alright Boys, show me what you got."

The added **boost** provided just enough juice.

The Twins were ready for the track.

Walter was first to heat his shoes.
He was confident he was not going to lose.

"Burmm WHINNEE
BURMPPPPPPPP
WHINEEBURRRRROOWWW
Chooooo,"

He left a big cloud of smoke
as he launched forward.

Now it was the Twins turn.

They couldn't wait to let their tires burn.

"Vroom Pop Pop

POP POP

Burmppppp

Chuwww..."

At the line,
they heard Walter's belt whine.

Walter's supercharger is
sounding really mean,
but the Twins are loading
2step boost into their
machine... when the light
flicks yellow and then
GREEN!!
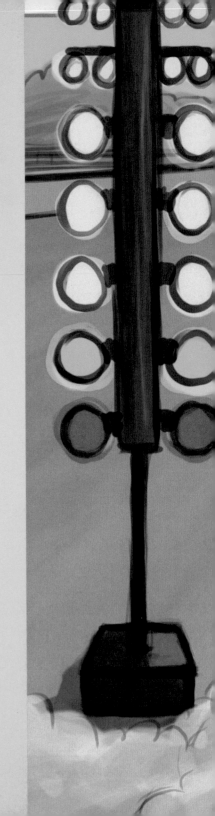

"SHHHWUSHHH CHUWWW SHWUSHHH WOMP WOMP POP POP POP POP POP."

"SKIRTTTTTT BURRRMMPPPPPPP CHUWWW BURMPPPPPPPPPPPPPPPPPPPPPPPPPPPPPPPPP"

The Twins scream off the line as they boost perfectly through every gear.

But what happened to Walter's supercharged motor was just what they feared.

He blew his motor
at the line...
it was not his day
to shine.

After a long successful race day,
Papa backed into the garage.
The Twins followed behind, it was
bedtime... time to unwind.

"I am very proud of you boys.
You had a great day, but remember
to relax and set your turbo timer."

The Twins set their timer for 30 seconds and the clock began to count down... 29... 28... 27... 26... A few moments later the Twin Snails were safe and sound... 5... 4... 3... 2... 1...

"Purmm"

Cool and comfortable, the boys fell asleep and silence once again filled the Motorhead Garage...

Look for more stories about The Twins' friends
at www.motorheadgarageproductions.com!

Made in the USA
Lexington, KY
13 August 2019